BECOMING A
STRETCHER BEARER
SELF STUDY MANUAL

MICHAEL SLATER

Cover design and layout by Rafael Polendo (polendo.net)
Cover images © mike_experto / Fotolia

Printed in the U.S.A.

CONTENTS

A WORD FROM PASTOR MIKE

"People who hurt are people on stretchers. To hurt is bad enough, but to hurt alone destroys people physically, mentally and spiritually."

The church of today desperately needs people who are willing to reach out and minister to their hurting friends. The knowledge of this truth has led me to begin and develop the practical ministry of "Stretcher Bearing", the Ministry of Encouragement and Support.

Paul exhorts us to "bear one another's burdens" (Galatians 6:2). We believe that most of us want to follow Paul's advice but are unable to because we simply don't know how. Stretcher Bearer Ministries will teach you how to reach out and minister to people on "stretchers". If you take the truths taught in this class and put them into action in your life and your church, you will begin to see a change in yourself and those around you. Instead of being paralyzed with inability to help a hurting friend, we will give you're the ability to creatively discover ways to reach out to those all around you.

I ask that before you take part in this class, you take a moment to pray for the Holy Spirit's leading in your life. Pray that you will begin to think of hurting people that you can reach, you can help. Pray that God will continue to bring people to your mind over the next few months and years that need their burdens carried, their stretchers lifted.

May God richly bless you as you minister and become a real Stretcher Bearer!

Encouraging One Another,

MIKE SLATER

PURPOSE

In this session we will become familiar with the concept of "Stretcher Bearing" and gain an understanding into the Biblical foundation of Encouragement and Support. We will also discover how to develop relationships of Encouragement!

The definition of a "Stretcher Bearer"

A person who _____ and _____ the gift of encouragement and support.

I. The Biblical Understanding of Encouragement

    A.   Mark 2:1-12; Understanding the "Stretcher Bearer" Concept

        1.   Pray for _____

        2.   Give of _____

    B.   Proverbs 18:24; "That Special Friend"

        1.   _____

        2.   _____

II. Insights Into Hurting People

    A.   What _____ people _____ necessarily being on a stretcher, but the sense that there is _____ that cares for me.

    B.   One time or another we _____ will experience being on a stretcher.

    C.   "Stretcher" times can happen when you will _____ expect it.

III.   Personal Study Time

A.   Jesus and the Gift of Encouragement
Look up the scripture references below and write a summary of how Jesus encouraged these people. Use the space provided to record your thought.

1.   John 8:1-11 _____

_____

_____

2.   Matthew 18:1-6 _____

_____

_____

3.   John 4:1-26 _____

_____

_____

4.   John 1:35-42 _____

_____

_____

5.   Mark 2:13-17 _____

_____

_____

6.   Acts 9 _____

_____

_____

7.   Matthew 16:13-20 _____

_____

_____

B. A Biblical Understanding of Support

Below are Old and New Testament references that will help you to understand the concept of supporting one another. Look up the scripture and summarize your thoughts in the space provided.

1. I Samuel 18 _____

_____

_____

_____

2. Exodus 17 _____

_____

_____

_____

3. Galatians 6:1-2 _____

_____

_____

_____

4. II Timothy 1:1-3 _____

_____

_____

_____

5. I Peter 5:13 _____

_____

_____

6. Matthew 26:36-45 _____

_____

_____

_____

IV. Personal Time

    A.   Who is your "special friend" shown in Proverbs 18:24? _____

_____

_____

_____

    B.   Do you think anyone would write your name as their "special friend"? Why or why not? _____

_____

_____

_____

    C.   Who would be the four people to carry your stretcher?

        1. _____

        2. _____

        3. _____

        4. _____

    D.   Analyze the contributions both you and your "Stretcher Bearers" have made to your relationships. What have you contributed to the friendship?

        1. _____

_____

        2. _____

_____

        3. _____

_____

        4. _____

_____

What contributions have your friends made to the relationship?

1. _____

_____

2. _____

_____

3. _____

_____

4. _____

_____

V.   Grab A Handle!

I encourage you to make contact with the friends you have listed and verbally express your feelings with them and share what they mean to you as a "Stretcher Bearer".

PURPOSE

This session deals with the questions and issues people face and why they often refuse to reach out for help and support. Why is it so hard for some to admit they need Support and Encouragement? We will learn to demonstrate to those around us that a "Stretcher Bearer" relationship can provide the trust that is necessary to be vulnerable in times of need.

I. Biblical Understanding - Mark 9:17-24 _____

_____

_____

_____

_____

_____

_____

_____

_____

_____

_____

II. Reasons Many Refuse to Admit They Need Help

    A.   Fear of being _____

    B.   Fear of _____

    C.   _____

    D.   Guilt of _____

III.   Let's Get Together

A.   Why do you think it is so hard for people to admit that they need to be supported or encouraged?

_____

_____

_____

_____

_____

_____

_____

_____

B.   Why do people feel threatened?

_____

_____

_____

_____

_____

_____

_____

_____

C.   When the father in Mark's passage in the Bible exclaims, "I do believe, help me in my unbelief", he displays what might be termed the "guilt of faithlessness". Why is this such a problem for many Christians?

_____

_____

_____

_____

_____

_____

_____

IV. Personal Time

A.   Take some time right now to think of people that you know who are on "stretchers" and refuse help. Identify the issues that keep them from seeking help and list ways in which you can develop trust.

<u>Friend</u>   <u>Issue</u>   <u>Ways I Can Build Trust</u>

1. _____   _____   _____
   _____
   _____
   _____

2. _____   _____   _____
   _____
   _____
   _____

3. _____   _____   _____
   _____
   _____
   _____

4. _____   _____   _____
   _____
   _____
   _____

5. _____   _____   _____
   _____
   _____
   _____

B.   What are some of the issues that hinder you from reaching out for help? List corrections you could make.

<u>My Issues</u>   <u>How I Can Improve</u>

1. _____   _____

    _____   _____

    _____   _____

2. _____   _____

    _____   _____

    _____   _____

3. _____   _____

    _____   _____

    _____   _____

V. Grab A Handle!

Close in silent prayer on behalf of someone you think might be "drowning". Ask God to open the door for you to minister and reach out to this person. May God bless you as you minister!

PURPOSE

Many times we find ourselves on a "stretcher" without the support of family and friends. Here we will determine how we can follow our Lord's example in order to find victory in difficult times. We also want to respond to the challenge of standing firm in our faith during these lonely times that we call "Gethsemane Moments".

I. An Understanding and Background into Gethsemane (Matthew 26:36-46) _____

_____

_____

_____

_____

_____

_____

II. A Practical Definition of "Gethsemane Moments"

The _____ places in life we _____

to face and many times _____.

III.   Keys to Handling the Hard Times

A.   _____

1.   What hinders obedience?

a.   Spirit vs. _____

b.   Here lies the grand _____ of life!

B.   _____

C. The key to obedience is the _____

   1.   No shortening of the race.

   2.   God will not _____ you in "Gethsemane". (Luke 22:43)

IV. Personal Time

   A.   Think of a time in your life that you would consider a "Gethsemane Moment". _____

   _____

   _____

   _____

   _____

   _____

   _____

   B.   How did you grow or what did you learn from your "Gethsemane Moment"? _____

   _____

   _____

   _____

   _____

   _____

   _____

   C.   Which keys do you find the *hardest to turn* in your life?

                    <u>Key</u>   <u>Why?</u>

   _____   _____

   _____   _____

   _____   _____

   _____   _____

How can you strengthen that key? _____

_____

_____

_____

_____

_____

_____

D.   How do you feel when you're alone - an "outsider"? _____

_____

_____

_____

_____

_____

_____

E.   How do you feel when you're part of a caring group? _____

_____

_____

_____

_____

_____

_____

V. Grab A Handle!

Close in prayer. Ask God to strengthen those people who are going through "Gethsemane Moments" and to use you to be what He calls you to be, a "Stretcher Bearer".

PURPOSE

We are meant to be people who love and care for one another. In our challenge to be a Stretcher Bearer we must learn to remove the bandages of our hurting world. Our responsibility in ministry is to identify the issues God deals with and the issues that He wants us to handle.

I. The Story of Jesus and Lazarus (John 11) _____

_____

_____

_____

_____

II. An Important Insight

    A.   Jesus deals with _____

    B.   We support main issues and deal with the _____

III. Thoughts on Secondary Issues

    A.   Many times it is the secondary issues that _____

    B.   Secondary issues can _____ and to witnessing!

    C.   Our main area of _____

IV. Story of Lazarus

Main Issue	Secondary Issues
_____	_____
	_____
	_____

V. Original "Stretcher Bearer" Story

<u>Main Issue</u>   <u>Secondary Issues</u>

_____   _____

_____

_____

_____

VI. Personal Time:
    Whose bandages does God want you to remove?

<u>Name</u>   <u>Main Issue</u>   <u>Secondary Issues</u>

_____   _____   _____

_____

_____   _____   _____

_____

_____   _____   _____

_____   _____   _____

_____

V. Grab A Handle!
    Are you beginning to see how important you are in the lives of others? Are people beginning to come across your mind whom you know need encouragement? Grab a handle! You can do it! God bless you, Stretcher Bearer!

PURPOSE

During this session we will explore the price of being a "Stretcher Bearer" and analyze the benefits of investing ourselves in one another.

I. The Price

    A.   What might it *cost you* to be the person who could lift another's stretcher?

        1. _____

        2. _____

        3. _____

        4. _____

        5. _____

        6. _____

        7. _____

        8. _____

        9. _____

II. The Cost of Being a Stretcher Bearer

    A. _____

        1.   _____

        2.   _____

    B. _____

        1.   _____

        2.   _____

C. _____

D. _____

E. _____

F. _____

G. _____

H. _____

I. _____

III. Personal Time:

A. Are there cost factors you need to overcome? _____

_____

_____

_____

_____

B. Now take the time to look back in your Bible at Mark 2. Identify and discuss the cost factors in the *original* "Stretcher Bearer" story.

1. _____

2. _____

3. _____

4. _____

5. _____

PURPOSE

In this session we will review the foundational elements of "Stretcher Bearing" and show practical ways in which a person can live out this ministry, developing effective strategies to touch other's lives.

I.   The Three Foundations of Stretcher Bearing

A.   Pray for _____. Ask God to make you _____ of

people and their _____. Be Sensitive To:

       1.   Body Language
       2.   Feelings
       3.   Emotions
       4.   Listening
       5.   Facial Expressions
       6.   Attitudes
       7.   Absence

B.   Pray for _____

       1.   Through creativity, you can show someone in a unique way that you _____.

       2.   This is a means of _____ on your prayer for sensitivity.

C.   _____ the concept of Stretcher Bearing in your own life. In this way you can show

others you _____ need Encouragement and Support at times. It helps others not to feel

_____ when they may need a "Stretcher Bearer". We must allow

_____ to minister to us. When you feel the importance of "Stretcher

Bearing" in your life, you are then better prepared to be a "Stretcher Bearer" to others! Dr. Lloyd Ogilvie

summarized this the best when he said, *"Something has to happen to* _____ *before it can*

happen _____ *you."*

II. Practical Tips on Becoming a "Stretcher Bearer"

    A.   Write _____ of Encouragement and Support.

    B.   Encouragement _____

    C.   _____

    D.   _____ ministry.

    E.   _____ group.

    F.   Season of _____

    G.   _____

III. Closing Thoughts

I pray that our time together has shown you the power and potential of the Ministry of Encouragement and Support. I hope you see that this ministry affects the whole body of Christ and is a commitment to become unified and involved with one another.

You see, stretchers can be lifted! We just need someone to grab the handle! I truly pray that special person will be you. God bless you, "Stretcher Bearer". May the teachings that were shared not only work, but also return to you through the encouragement of others.

STRETCHER BEARER MINISTRIES

ADDITIONAL RESOURCE MATERIALS

The Book, *The Stretcher* $15

"Becoming A Stretcher Bearer" Self Study Manual $35
Includes workbook and entire seminar on CD

"Becoming A Stretcher Bearer" Audio Series... $20
Includes highlights from the seminar on CD

For more resources and to place an order, please visit our website.

SEMINAR INFORMATION

Pastor and author Michael Slater travels the U.S. speaking on the ministry of Support and Encouragement at churches, retreats, colleges, and organizations. For more information on our "Becoming A Stretcher Bearer" seminar or to book Pastor Mike for your next speaking engagement, please visit our website.

CONTACT INFORMATION

P.O. Box 1035
La Habra, California 90633-1035

(714) 869-1440 | mike@stretcherbearerministries.org

www.stretcherbearerministries.org

LaVergne, TN USA
10 March 2011
219512LV00001B/4/P

9 780983 204312